Book

for the

Commemoration

of the Living
and of the Dead

Printed with the blessing of His Eminence,
Metropolitan Hilarion, First Hierarch
of the Russian Orthodox Church
Outside of Russia

Book of Commemoration for the Living and the Dead
© 2014 Holy Trinity Monastery

The Prayer for Every Departed Person is copyright © 2011 by
David James - A Psalter for Prayer, trans. David James
(Jordanville, New York: Holy Trinity Publications, 2011)
ISBN 978-0-88465-188-8

HOLY TRINITY PUBLICATIONS
The Printshop of St Job of Pochaev
Holy Trinity Monastery
Jordanville, New York 13361-0036
www.holytrinitypublications.com

ISBN: 978-0-88465-378-3

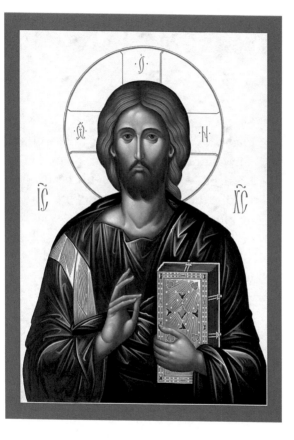

A Prayer for the Living

Save, O Lord, and have mercy on all Orthodox Christians in every place of Thy dominion. Grant unto them, O Lord, peace of soul and bodily health. Pardon them every sin, voluntary and involuntary, through the intercessions of Thy most pure Mother and of all Thy saints, and have mercy on me the wretched one.

For the health
and salvation of the servants of God:

_____

_____

_____

_____

_____

_____

_____

_____

For the health:

_____

_____

_____

_____

_____

_____

_____

_____

_____

_____

_____

_____

_____

_____

For the health:

For the health:

_____

_____

_____

_____

_____

_____

_____

_____

_____

_____

_____

_____

_____

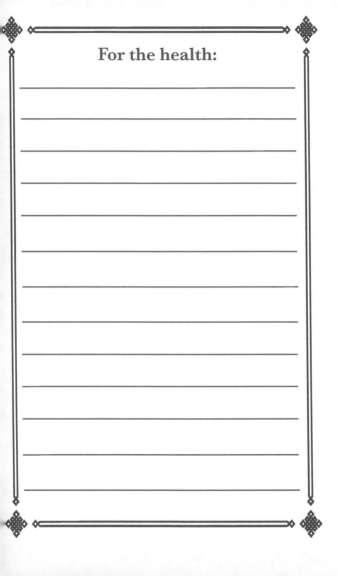

For the health:

For the health:

For the health:

For the health:

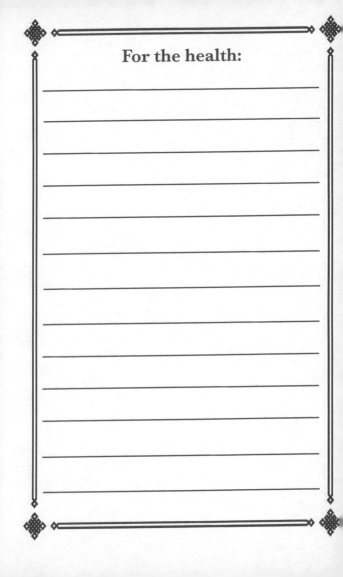

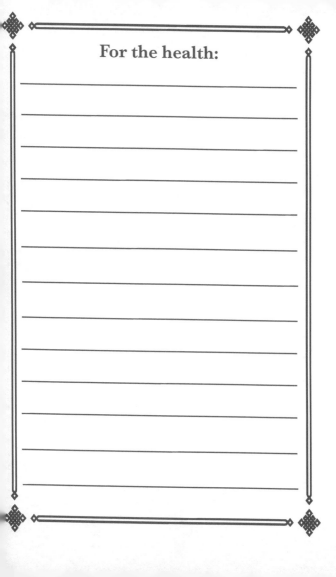

For the health:

_____

_____

_____

_____

_____

_____

_____

_____

_____

_____

_____

_____

_____

For the health:

For the health:

For the health:

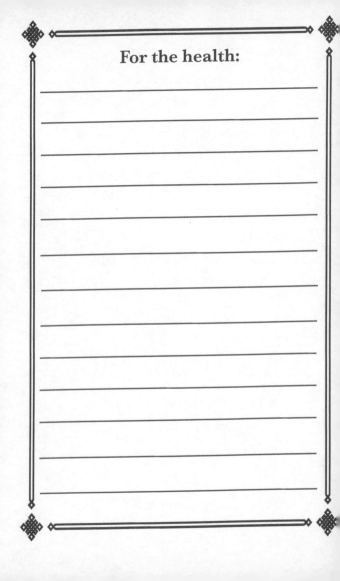

For the health:

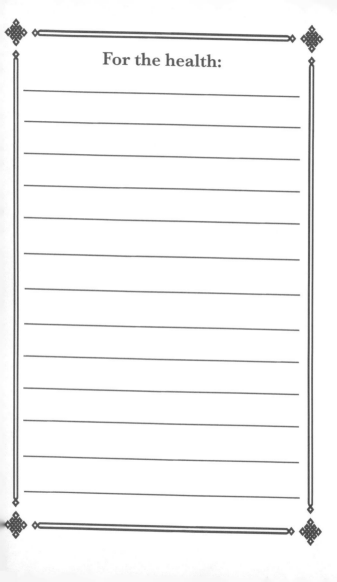

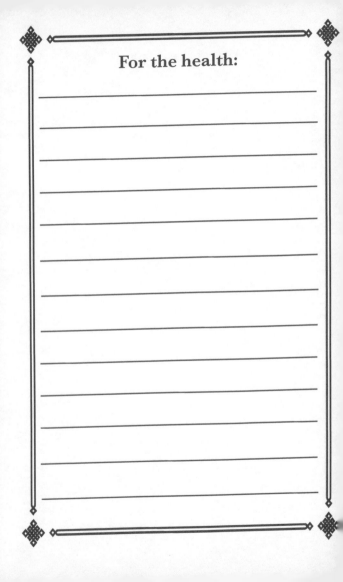

For the health:

For the health:

For the health:

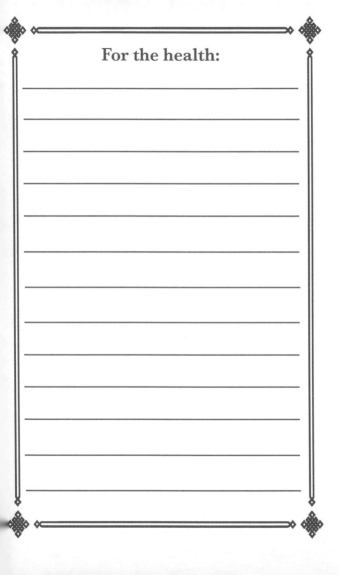

For the health:

_____

_____

_____

_____

_____

_____

_____

_____

_____

_____

_____

_____

_____

For the health:

_____

_____

_____

_____

_____

_____

_____

_____

_____

_____

_____

_____

_____

For the health:

For the health:

_____

_____

_____

_____

_____

_____

_____

_____

_____

_____

_____

_____

_____

For the health:

_____

_____

_____

_____

_____

_____

_____

_____

_____

_____

_____

_____

_____

_____

_____

_____

For the health:

_____

_____

_____

_____

_____

_____

_____

_____

_____

_____

_____

_____

_____

_____

For the health:

_____

_____

_____

_____

_____

_____

_____

_____

_____

_____

_____

_____

_____

For the Repose
of the
Servants of God

ВОСКРЕСЕНІЕ ХРТОВО

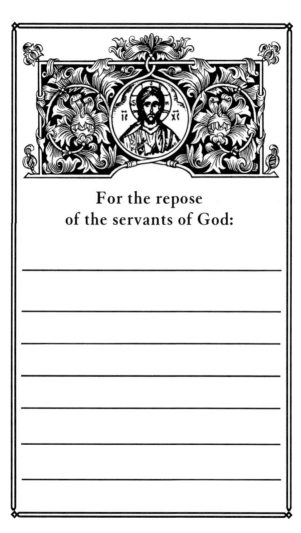

For the repose
of the servants of God:

_____

_____

_____

_____

_____

_____

_____

For the repose:

_____

_____

_____

_____

_____

_____

_____

_____

_____

_____

_____

For the repose:

_____

_____

_____

_____

_____

_____

_____

_____

_____

_____

_____

For the repose:

_____

_____

_____

_____

_____

_____

_____

_____

_____

_____

_____

For the repose:

_____

_____

_____

_____

_____

_____

_____

_____

_____

_____

_____

_____

For the repose:

_____

_____

_____

_____

_____

_____

_____

_____

_____

_____

_____

For the repose:

_____

_____

_____

_____

_____

_____

_____

_____

_____

_____

_____

For the repose:

_____

_____

_____

_____

_____

_____

_____

_____

_____

_____

_____

_____

For the repose:

_____

_____

_____

_____

_____

_____

_____

_____

_____

_____

_____

For the repose:

_____

_____

_____

_____

_____

_____

_____

_____

_____

_____

_____

For the repose:

_____

_____

_____

_____

_____

_____

_____

_____

_____

_____

For the repose:

_____

_____

_____

_____

_____

_____

_____

_____

_____

_____

_____

For the repose:

_____

_____

_____

_____

_____

_____

_____

_____

_____

_____

_____

For the repose:

For the repose:

_____

_____

_____

_____

_____

_____

_____

_____

_____

_____

_____

PRAYER
For Every Departed Person

REMEMBER, O Lord our God, Thy servant [handmaiden] who hath departed in the faith and hope of eternal life, our brother [sister], [N.], and, as Thou art good and lovest mankind, pardon his [her] sins and consume his [her] unrighteousness; release, remit and forgive all his [her] sins, voluntary and involuntary. Deliver him [her] from eternal torment and from the fire of Gehenna, and grant unto him [her] participation and enjoyment of Thine eternal blessings, which have been prepared for them that love Thee. For if [s]he sinned, yet [s]he did not renounce Thee and believed undoubtingly in Thee as God: the Father, the Son, and the Holy Spirit, glorified in Trinity, and confessed the Unity in Trinity and the Trinity in Unity in Orthodox fashion, even until his [her] last breath. Therefore, be merciful unto him [her], and impute his [her] faith in Thee of the Soul instead of deeds and, as One gracious, grant unto him [her] rest with Thy saints. For there is no man who liveth and sinneth not, and Thou only art without sin, and Thy righteousness is righteousness for ever. For Thou alone art a God of mercy, and compassion, and love for mankind, and unto Thee do we ascribe glory, to the Father, and to the Son, and to the Holy Spirit; now, and ever, and unto the ages of ages. Amen.